Leading As a Friend

John C. Maxwell
Leadership Books for Students

(Based on *Developing the Leader Within You*)

Leading from the Lockers:
Student Edition

ISBN 0-8499-7722-3

Leading from the Lockers:
Guided Journal

ISBN 0-8499-7723-1

The PowerPak Series

Leading Your Sports Team

ISBN 0-8499-7725-8

Leading in Your Youth Group

ISBN 0-8499-7726-6

Leading at School

ISBN 0-8499-7724-X

Leading As a Friend

ISBN 0-8499-7727-4

"These books are outstanding. John Maxwell's leadership principles have been communicated in a way that any student can understand and practice. Take them and go make a difference in your world."

—Dr. Tim Elmore,
Vice President of Leadership Development, EQUIP;
Author of *Nurturing the Leader in Your Child*

Leading As a Friend

by
John C. Maxwell

with
Mark Littleton

Tommy nelson®
Thomas Nelson, Inc. • Nashville

POWERPAK SERIES: LEADING AS A FRIEND

Based on John C. Maxwell's *Developing the Leader Within You.*

Published in Nashville, Tennessee, by Tommy Nelson®, a division of Thomas Nelson, Inc.

Special thanks to Ron Luce and Teen Mania for providing research materials for this book.

Unless otherwise indicated, Scripture quotations are from the *International Children's Bible, New Century Version,* copyright © 1983, 1986, 1988.

Scripture quotations marked (NKJV) are from the NEW KING JAMES VERSION of the Bible, copyright © 1979, 1980, 1982, Thomas Nelson, Inc., Publishers.

Library of Congress Cataloging-in-Publication Data

Maxwell, John C., 1947–
  Leading as a friend / John C. Maxwell with Mark Littleton.
    p. cm. — (PowerPak collection)
  "Based on John C. Maxwell's Developing the leader within you"—
T.p. verso.
    ISBN 0-8499-7727-4
    1. Leadership—Religious aspects—Christianity—Juvenile literature.
2. Friendship—Religious aspects—Christianity—Juvenile literature. [1.
Leadership—Religious aspects—Christianity. 2. Christian life.
3. Conduct of life.] I. Littleton, Mark R., 1950– II. Maxwell John C.,
1947– Developing the leader within you. III. Title. IV. Series.

BV4597.53.L43 L58 2001
248.8'3—dc21

                                                                  2001031493

Printed in the United States of America

01 02 03 04 05 PHX 5 4 3 2 1

Contents

1
Wanted:
Young Leaders

What a Friend I Have in You

Lenny didn't have many friends. Most kids avoided him. He seemed to be very quiet and dressed differently from the other kids. One day, Fred noticed Lenny was always alone. Fred had decided to take seriously the idea of building friendships for the kingdom of God and possibly leading those friends to Christ and into a close walk with Him. He sat down at Lenny's lunch table, where Lenny was munching on a sub sandwich.

"Hey," Fred said as he sat down nearby. Lenny responded by turning away.

"Want some chips? I have two bags," Fred said, pushing a small bag of chips toward Lenny.

Looking at the chips with curiosity, Lenny turned to stare into Fred's eyes. "What do you want?" he muttered.

"Just thought you might like some chips is all," he said. "I'm Fred."

"Flintstone?" Lenny said.

Fred cracked up. "Yeah, I get that a lot. No, actually it's Martin. Nothing spectacular."

They ate in silence. Fred finished his lunch and said, "Well, see you tomorrow." And he started to leave.

Lenny grabbed Fred's arm. "What do you want?"

"A friend," Fred said.

"Why me?"

"Why not?"

Lenny stared up at Fred with skeptical but sad eyes. "Everybody wants something."

Fred shrugged. "I like to make friends."

Before Lenny could answer, Fred turned and walked to the trash cans.

Later that afternoon, he said hello to Lenny

in the hall and then spotted him again on the way to the bus.

That day marked the small beginning of a great friendship. Lenny became a Christian six months later, joined Fred's youth group, and built other friendships along the way. Lenny later told Fred that the day Fred approached him in the lunchroom had been a low point in his life. He was new at the school and didn't fit in with the rest of the students. He was thinking about dropping out, maybe even running away from home. Lenny's whole life changed, all because one guy thought leading as a friend was important. And guess what! Fred's life changed, too. He gained a lifelong friend and found the way God wanted him to lead.

> JEREMIAH 1:6: "BUT LORD GOD, I DON'T KNOW HOW TO SPEAK. I AM ONLY A BOY."
> —JEREMIAH TO GOD

Take Me to Your Leader

Perhaps more than at any other time in history, we need leaders among today's youth. We need you! Television, CDs, video and computer games, the

Internet—all beckon for attention. All can sway people to waste time, money, and their lives on foolishness, or they can enlighten and teach.

But we need leaders to show the way. For example: Cassie Bernall switched on a school with her quiet testimony of faith in the face of death. Her commitment has paved the way for many others to follow in life. Many teens today have committed themselves to the "TRUE LOVE WAITS" philosophy of keeping themselves sexually pure until marriage. It started with a leader.

Other teens have organized rallies, led campaigns in various cities, and raised up a new crop of Christians through friendship evangelism. It began because someone decided to step out and lead.

Such leaders are even more necessary when it comes to friendship.

☐ Without leaders in their lives, your friends will possibly be enticed to follow the ways of the world and the devil rather than those of Christ.

☐ Without caring leaders, your friends will not care, either.

☐ **Without enthusiastic and committed leaders, friends at every level will stray into temptation and possibly failure.**

But with caring and enthusiastic leaders, anything is possible. Christ is shared. Lives are changed. Families come together.

A Friend in Deed

Maybe you're thinking, *My friends don't want me to lead them. They just want to have a good time.*

You may think of leading as being president of the youth group or captain of the football team. But in reality, your closest friends are the ones most likely to respond to your leadership, if you define it properly. At its most basic level, LEADERSHIP IS SIMPLY TOUCHING OTHERS FOR GOOD, FOR GROWTH, AND FOR GOD. Merely nudging your friends in the right direction when they're thinking of doing something wrong is a hallmark of leadership.

That's right. You don't have to stand out in

the backyard and cry, "Follow me, people! I know where to take you!" That would be laughable. But if you think of leadership as subtly making suggestions, helping your friends make wise decisions, and offering advice when necessary, you're leading well.

What are the benefits of such leadership?

☐ You receive respect from your friends.

☐ You learn to give respect to your friends.

☐ You have the satisfaction of knowing you helped your friends at crucial points in their lives.

☐ You could be the reason they become or stay Christians.

☐ You could receive the reward of a heartfelt thanks and possibly more.

☐ You become well prepared for leading in your adult years.

Ultimately, the most respected, most remembered, and most revered people are those considered leaders. Think of Andrew in John 1 going to his brother Simon and leading

Great Leaders Who Started Working with Friends

Ronald Reagan
(former president of
the United States)

George H. W. Bush
(former president of
the United States)

Rebecca
St. James
(musician)

John F. Kennedy
(former president of
the United States)

Michelle Akers
(Olympian and soccer
champion)

Josh McDowell
(youth leader
and evangelist)

Michael W. Smith
(musician)

Tiger Woods
(pro golfer)

him to Christ; through that, Simon became Peter, the Rock. Think of Paul befriending Timothy and leading him into the ministry. The letters Paul wrote to Timothy still have effects on us today. Think of any great person and you will undoubtedly find friends in their history who led them at important crossroads. The young people you know today will grow up to be the leaders of tomorrow, and now is your chance to leave a mark on them for God.

Walk with the Master

Jesus wants to fill your life with great qualities such as love, joy, peace, and faithfulness. It's part of your Christian walk with Him. Jesus wants to make you a leader. He proclaims He will make you a "fisherman of men," if you let Him—and possibly a leader in your home and extended family, church, school, community, and government.

Would you consider being a leader? Would you gladly step up to the mark and run that race for God's kingdom?

Every person has the potential to be a leader as a friend. You're not striving to be the leader of your country, but to have a positive effect on the lives of your friends.

You never know what God will do. He has a way of zeroing in on people you'd never expect.

Who would have thought the twelve disciples Jesus chose would become the world-changers they did? Or Jonah? Or David? Or even Moses? God sees beneath the surface. He sees the heart and He knows right now what is in your heart. He knows the leader He'd like you to be!

Made in the Shade with a Lemonade

You may think, *But I'm not good at this. People won't follow me! They'll laugh at me—that's what they'll do. Laugh at me!*

Really? Are you sure? That's what Dalia thought. So, she tended to sit at the back of classes,

In Your Christian Walk

- ☐ You will become more like Jesus. (Romans 8:29)
- ☐ You will have the opportunity to share your faith. (2 Timothy 4:2–5)
- ☐ You could become bold for the kingdom of God. (Colossians 4:2–6)
- ☐ God will open doors for you all over. (Revelation 3:8)

watch, and keep quiet. Then one day, in a way that surprised even her, she became a leader.

Dalia went with a friend to a party. When they got there, it wasn't as they'd expected. There were some things that made Dalia uneasy. **Drugs. Booze. Sex.**

Dalia had strong beliefs against using drugs or drinking alcohol. And she didn't believe in sex before marriage. But she and her friend had never talked about it. Someone walked in with a bunch of six-packs, offering everyone a beer. Her friend took one. Dalia refused.

Several members of the group looked at Dalia and in unison said, "Whatsamatta—chicken?"

"No," Dalia said. "It's stupid."

The group looked at the two girls and went on with their party.

Her friend set down her beer without drinking it. Then someone began passing around drugs. This time Dalia didn't hesitate. "No thanks," she said, and took it out of her friend's hand. "That's dangerous. Don't do it."

Her friend gazed at her, then shrugged. "Yeah, Dalia, you're right. Let's get out of here, before it gets worse."

Great Leaders Who Almost Weren't

Moses—killed an Egyptian, then spent the next forty years regretting it until God called him at the burning bush.

Habakkuk—just a guy with a lot of questions until the answers became a book of the Bible.

David—King Saul repeatedly tried to kill him, but God kept him safe until the time was right.

Mary Magdalene—possessed by seven demons, but when Jesus cast them out, she became possessed by His love and power.

Esther—the prettiest girl in Babylon, she used her looks and her wits to save Israel at the risk of her own life.

Lydia—just another businesswoman, until she met Paul and her life was changed forever.

The group laughed at them, with the exception of one girl. She refused, too, and set down her beer. As the girls got ready to leave, she did, too.

On the way home, her friend said, "Thanks, Dalia. I wouldn't have had the guts to say no if you hadn't."

2 CHRONICLES 16:9: THE LORD SEARCHES ALL THE EARTH FOR PEOPLE WHO HAVE GIVEN THEMSELVES COMPLETELY TO HIM. HE WANTS TO MAKE THEM STRONG.

That simple situation called for leadership. And Dalia stepped up to the plate.

God wants you to be a leader, and He'll give you what you need to make it happen—courage, faith, commitment, skill. . . .

GOD WILL USE YOU IF YOU LET HIM. THE QUESTION IS: WILL YOU LET HIM?

2
Influence:
You Can't Lead without It

What is leadership? Leadership is *influence*. When you influence people to change a course of action, to choose to do what's right over what's wrong, or simply to follow the Scriptures on a point of practice, you're leading.

"I'm Amazed. They Did What I Said!"

To be a leader you'll need followers, but how do you get followers? By influence. As you talk about a plan, as you try to persuade others to take a course of action, as you talk a friend out of doing something that might harm him or her, you're influencing that person.

In fact, you're probably influencing people for good or for bad all the time, whether you know it or not.

In Flew Ence

Think of a guy named Ence. Okay, it's a little dumb. But when everyone was standing

How Do You Influence Friends?

☐ By providing them confidence through your emotional support

☐ By listening

☐ By cheering them on

☐ By getting everyone involved

☐ By getting people to complete something when they'd rather quit

☐ By revealing a new idea when everyone else is stymied

☐ By reading Scripture with them

around the backyard not knowing what to do when Bill broke his leg, Ence took charge. He flew into action and got things rolling toward getting an ambulance for Bill. It was simple: *In flew Ence.* Influence.

Okay, maybe that's a bit on the weird side, but if influence is anything it's jumping into action while everyone else is standing still.

And You Never Know Who Will Fly with You!

The amazing thing about influence is that you never know who will go with you.

In the movie *Gladiator,* Maximus, at one time a great Roman general, is betrayed and ends up a gladiator. Now, those boys were generally loners, fighting for their survival against everyone else. But Maximus used his leadership skills to join that little band of loners together to fight some of the greatest fighters in the Roman games—and win. Maximus had no idea whether he could get anyone to follow him in the games, but he knew his own survival required that he try. He did. And won.

Fishing for People

If you're like me, you probably want to influence your friends so that they will join God's team. After all, that's what it's ultimately about.

But you say to me, "I'm no Maximus. I'm no great leader."

Sure, but you are a child of God. You belong to God's kingdom. Therefore, God wants to

A King Who Failed As a Leader

You probably know the story of King Saul. Appointed by God as king, Saul made some terrible errors by forgetting God at crucial moments. Eventually, God decided to select a new king, David, because King Saul was so disobedient. Saul failed as God's leader, not because he didn't have ability or even the people's trust, but because he failed to obey God at important crossroads.

Make sure you obey God as a leader, and all will be well.

give you a chance at excelling for Him. He may pick you to lead in a situation you've never thought about, just like Maximus.

2 TIMOTHY 1:7: GOD DID NOT GIVE US A SPIRIT THAT MAKES US AFRAID. HE GAVE US A SPIRIT OF POWER AND LOVE AND SELF-CONTROL.

Be available, let God know you're willing, learn all you can about leadership, and then leave the rest to Him. You'll be surprised when He gets you to fly in and make things happen.

Start at Square One

Everyone begins leading at some level. Some people gain a *position* of leadership by being elected to it. Some are appointed. Others win support and gain followers, who thrust them into it. As Shakespeare said, "Some are born great. Some attain greatness. And some have greatness thrust upon them."

It happens all kinds of ways. What you want to be sure of is that however you become a leader to your friends, you eventually win their trust. They follow you not because you live across the street from each other, but because they know you care about them and will always do what's right.

I'll Follow You Wherever You Want to Go!

One of the great friendships of the Bible was between Naomi and Ruth. They both lost their husbands in a foreign land. Ruth's husband had been Naomi's son. At one point, Naomi decided to return to the land of Israel, her homeland, and she told her two daughters-in-law, Orpah and Ruth, to stay in Moab, their homeland. Orpah agreed, but Ruth clung to Naomi. She said she'd go wherever Naomi went because she loved Naomi.

> "IF YOU SMILE WHEN NOBODY ELSE IS AROUND, YOU REALLY MEAN IT."
>
> —ANDY ROONEY, 60 MINUTES

That is precisely what Ruth did. Her love not only won over Naomi, but also a man named Boaz, who would become Ruth's husband.

That is really the essence of leading as a

friend. It involves trust, love, commitment, and loyalty. When you're like that with your friends, you will be able to lead them because they will want to be led.

Helping Friends with Choices

Cloe and Tomi lived near each other in the same neighborhood. They had been friends since they were toddlers. As they grew up, they shared many experiences. Cloe, however, became a Christian at age thirteen. Tomi's parents had no particular religion and didn't care about it.

Naturally, Cloe began inviting Tomi to church. In time, Tomi also accepted Christ. But the real depth of their friendship was cemented when Tomi decided she'd accept a date with Bob, a guy Cloe didn't like or trust. She tried to persuade Tomi not to go out with Bob, but Tomi said he

1 TIMOTHY 4:12: YOU ARE YOUNG, BUT DO NOT LET ANYONE TREAT YOU AS IF YOU WERE NOT IMPORTANT. BE AN EXAMPLE TO SHOW THE BELIEVERS HOW THEY SHOULD LIVE.

Jesus, the Greatest Leader of All

Jesus started off in the classic place of leadership: He was appointed by His Father. At Jesus' baptism, God declared in a booming voice, "This is My beloved Son, in whom I am well pleased." (Matthew 3:17 NKJV)

That was an intriguing way to begin, but just having Dad say you're a leader isn't usually enough. Jesus won His followers through doing miracles, speaking great words of hope and love, and by guiding them through tough territory. They followed Him in the end because they wanted to, not because Jesus lived on the same street.

That's ultimately the reason you will want any of your friends to follow you.

was "hot" and was the number one guy in the freshman class.

The night before Tomi and Bob's date, Cloe and Tomi went to a party. Bob was there. Tomi promptly disappeared with Bob. Cloe danced with another guy, Pascal, but she kept watching

JEREMIAH 29:11: "I SAY THIS BECAUSE I KNOW WHAT I HAVE PLANNED FOR YOU," SAYS THE LORD. "I HAVE GOOD PLANS FOR YOU. I DON'T PLAN TO HURT YOU. I PLAN TO GIVE YOU HOPE AND A GOOD FUTURE."

for Tomi. Finally, worried that something had happened, she asked Pascal to help her find Tomi. They asked around and learned Bob had taken Tomi upstairs to a bedroom.

Cloe and Pascal ran up the stairs and stormed into one room after another until they found Tomi struggling as Bob attempted to rape her!

Cloe and Pascal managed to pummel Bob until he let Tomi go. Then Pascal, Tomi, and Cloe rushed downstairs and called Cloe's mom.

When you lead as a friend, you watch out for your friends. When they're vulnerable, you take the steps you need to help and, if necessary, save them from disaster.

3
The Power of Priorities

Jerome had so many things to do. Go to youth group. Prepare a speech for literature class. Talk to his small group and lead it. Finish his chores at home. Have a quiet time. Get dressed. Brush his teeth. . . .

Oh, man. Does it ever end? How is he going to fit in everything?

Jerome's problem is one we all have. How do we fit in all the things we have to do today, this week, this year?

For Jerome to function effectively as a leader, he has to master his schedule and thus his time. He needs to decide: What's important? What's

Christian Goals

THERE ARE MANY GOALS YOU CAN HAVE IN LIFE. THESE ARE IMPORTANT, IF YOU ARE GOING TO GROW IN YOUR FAITH IN CHRIST.

- ☐ Have a real relationship with God on a daily basis.
- ☐ Become a true disciple who knows what and why he believes what he believes.
- ☐ Become more like Jesus day by day.
- ☐ Challenge others to consider Christ.

more important? What's *most* important?

If he can determine the answers to those questions, he will start giving himself to the things that matter. And he'll be able to leave the others till later or even let go of the things that don't matter. That's called setting priorities.

Whether you realize it or not, everything you do is governed by priorities. If you're not careful, you will give your time and attention to only the things that scream the loudest. When you operate at that level, all you begin to hear are the screams.

But creating priorities, writing items down on your "Top Ten" list of things to do today or this week, will enable you to make sure you do the things that matter.

How, then, do you begin prioritizing?

Think of all the goals the Bible has laid out for you. Which ones do you think are most important?

Don't Be Out of Order!

It comes down to one basic thing: organization.

It's really rather simple. Get yourself a piece of paper that you won't lose, something you can keep with you. Then begin writing down all the things you need to do that day. Don't worry about putting them in order or deciding which is most important. Just get the list made.

Once you've done that, start making choices. Select the three to six most important ones and then put them into some order of importance. For example, your list might look like this:

▢ FEED AND TAKE OUT THE DOG.

▢ CLEAN ROOM.

▢ PLAN DISCIPLESHIP GROUP MEETING.

▢ HAVE A QUIET TIME.

▢ PREPARE PEP TALK FOR YOUTH GROUP.

▢ PRAY.

▢ SPEND SOME TIME WITH JOHN (OR MARY, BILL, CINDY, OR WHOMEVER).

Now look at the list. Which ones should you do first today? What order would you put them in by way of importance?

3. FEED AND TAKE OUT THE DOG.

7. CLEAN ROOM.

4. PLAN DISCIPLESHIP GROUP MEETING.

1. HAVE A QUIET TIME.

5. PREPARE PEP TALK FOR YOUTH GROUP.

2. PRAY.

6. SPEND SOME TIME WITH JOHN (OR MARY, BILL, CINDY, OR WHOMEVER).

You should plan these things according to the time of day you would best do them and go from there. For instance, spending time with John is very important, but it's number six on the list because you can't do it till he gets home from school at, say, four o'clock. You can do all those other things before then.

EPHESIANS 5:15: BE VERY CAREFUL HOW YOU LIVE. DO NOT LIVE LIKE THOSE WHO ARE NOT WISE. LIVE WISELY.

Do you see the power of such a list? Suddenly you're ORGANIZED! You have some goals to strive for. You have a plan of action. You're going to accomplish something incredible today!

Pull That Rip Cord

Making choices is what life is all about. Every day you will have tens—if not hundreds—of little choices. For instance, you're about to have your quiet time when the thought comes into your head, *Why not have a snack?* Or, *Should I check out that new video game?*

Choosing to Serve

The apostle Paul had many choices before him as a follower of Christ. He could go to the market and buy beans. He could run down to the temple and listen to a great teacher. He could take a trip to Joppa and sit on the beach. Instead, Paul chose to go out into the world and try to start churches by leading people to Christ. That became his number one priority. As a result, on three missionary journeys he traveled to much of the Roman world and planted churches wherever he went. He became the greatest missionary who has ever been.

Why?

Because he had a priority: **Preach the gospel everywhere you go.**

Choices! Now, if you have priorities for your day, you've already made some choices. You say no to the snack and the video game because you've prioritized. You've already decided what is most important for that moment. You don't have to hesitate, hem and haw around, or go back and forth. No, you say, "Now is the time for my quiet time. Nothing else intrudes."

Later, you might be tempted to go to the mall or watch a movie, but your priority of spending time with John comes into the picture. Now you have something you want to accomplish, so you say no to the other things and spend time with John.

Remember: Priorities put you in control of your time and your life. You're no longer spinning your wheels. You're going somewhere, and you're going to accomplish some great things.

But God Wants So Much!

Of course, sooner or later you'll have to ask the question: What does God really want me to do? What's the goal of this year, my time in high school?

Knowing God's will is a tough issue for many Christians. But it's really rather simple. To find out God's will for you:

☐ Read the Bible. And as you read, ask yourself, "How can I apply this to my life?"

☐ Spend time in prayer. Ask God, "What do You want me to do? What are Your goals for me this year?" He will answer if you're willing to listen.

☐ Seek others' opinions. Ask yourself, "What about my parents, friends, and leaders? What do they have to say that might help me?"

☐ Consider your situation. Ask yourself, "Does my situation point me in the right direction? Do I need to change? Reevaluate my goals? Learn a new skill to reach my goals?"

You Can't Fish with a Bare Hook

Finding out God's will is a lot like fishing. When you fish, what do you do? You bait the hook, throw it out, and see what happens.

In knowing God's will, the bait is your commitment to Christ. "Lord," you say to Him, "I want to know Your will. So I'm throwing out a hook. Show me what to do."

Say you're wondering if God wants you to take a certain course, build a friendship with a certain person, or get involved in a certain club. You throw out your hook—talk to a counselor about the course, strike up a conversation with the person, or go to the club—and see what happens. If God is leading you, He might give you a strike. You get signed up for the course. The person gets interested, and you talk more. The club is more interesting to you.

> "SET PRIORITIES FOR YOUR GOALS. A MAJOR PART OF SUCCESSFUL LIVING LIES IN THE ABILITY TO PUT FIRST THINGS FIRST . . . THE REASON MOST MAJOR GOALS ARE NOT ACHIEVED IS THAT WE SPEND OUR TIME DOING SECOND THINGS FIRST."
>
> —ROBERT J. McKAIN, AUTHOR

Maybe those are God's ways of saying, "This is what I want you to do."

Open doors (or biting fish) aren't the only

COLOSSIANS 3:16: LET THE TEACHING OF CHRIST LIVE IN YOU RICHLY. USE ALL WISDOM TO TEACH AND STRENGTHEN EACH OTHER.

ways God communicates. Sometimes a door closes at first, but then opens as you keep knocking. It all depends on how much you want to do something. If you want to build a friendship with so-and-so, but you keep on getting the brush-off, then maybe God is saying, "Try someone else."

4

Being Who You Really Are without Pretending

Rhonda sat down with her friends at lunch. "Did you hear what the idiot did today?"

"Ellie?" one of her friends asked.

"What other idiot do you know?"

"What?" everyone clamored.

"She went up to Mr. Oldham and told him she'd be willing to clean the floor in the gym if some others would help her."

"What a jerk!"

"She's always doing that kind of stuff. She is an idiot."

At that moment, Ellie walked over and sat down.

"Hey," Rhonda said to her, "I hear you're helping with the gym problem. That's really cool."

Ellie grinned. "I just need three others, and we've got it done."

Ever seen a situation like that one? Someone is one person to your face and another one behind your back. We have a name for such people: **TWO-FACED**. It matches perfectly. They put on one face for some people and another face for others. It's one of the worst forms of dishonesty and lack of integrity.

MATTHEW 5:16: YOU SHOULD BE A LIGHT FOR OTHER PEOPLE. LIVE SO THAT THEY WILL SEE THE GOOD THINGS YOU DO. LIVE SO THAT THEY WILL PRAISE YOUR FATHER IN HEAVEN.

If you want to lead as a friend, you have to leave the whole two-faced thing behind once and for all and never let it infect you again. Real leaders are people who are honest, who have integrity.

What is integrity? It's being who you really are on the inside and letting it show on the outside. It's never playing games, never lying, never pretending to be something you aren't.

If you want to build real friendships that last, integrity in them is most important. Only through integrity can you build the kind of trust that makes for real friendship.

Honesty is not a trick or a strategy. It's a lifestyle. Integrity is not what we do but who we are, and who we are determines what we do.

Putting the "Amen" in "Amends"

After I made my commitment to Christ, my life changed dramatically. In fact, I realized I had to make some things right. First, I had to go to Mr. Galliher of Galliher's Drug Store and confess that I had stolen a sports magazine. I was totally embarrassed. I paid for the magazine and waited for his response. Fortunately, he was gracious and forgave me.

My next stop was the grocery store not far away. It may seem small today, but I knew I had taken a Dr Pepper from the store. I offered to pay for it and apologized. The grocer, too, was very gracious to me. The more I did this, the easier I found it became.

My final stop was to visit one of my coaches in high school. I returned some practice jerseys,

People Who Had Integrity in the Bible

Daniel had so much integrity in his work that the king planned to put him in charge of his whole kingdom. Then when Daniel's enemies wanted to prevent the king from doing that, they looked for wrongdoings they could accuse him of—but they couldn't find any.

Nehemiah was a man such of integrity that he refused to be cruel to the people he ruled or to demand that they give him money and their food. Instead, he fed many of them fine meals that he was entitled to as governor of Judah.

Paul was a man of such integrity that his followers trusted him to tell them only the truth and God trusted him to write it.

Hosea was a man of such great integrity that even when his wife committed adultery, he forgave her and continued to love her.

Jesus had the most integrity of anyone, so much so that no one could convict Him of any sin.

a ball, and a towel. I had taken them during my last two years of playing on the team. I just didn't feel right knowing I had these things. Somehow I knew that if I wanted to be effective and keep a clear conscience in my life—I had to make things right and keep them right! (By the way, all of these gentlemen expressed how pleased they were with me.)

Keeping the Bar High

How do you build integrity into your life? By having high standards. When you are a person of integrity, people notice. They say things like, "What you see is what you get with him," "I've never caught her lying. She always tells the truth," and "You can trust him. He won't fake you out."

EPHESIANS 4:15:
WE WILL SPEAK THE TRUTH WITH LOVE.

Without integrity you can't lead others because they'll never trust you.

Lack of Integrity Destroys Friends

The story of Cain and Abel is familiar to most of us, but one thing we may have missed was the real problem between them. Abel obeyed God and brought God the best of his flock as a sacrifice of thanks for God's blessings. Cain, being a farmer, thought he'd skimp and only brought the useless, worthless vegetables to God. When God rejected it and Cain complained to Abel, Abel spoke the truth, advising Cain to bring the best. Cain didn't like it. His lack of integrity in a sacrifice led to another sin: the murder of his brother.

The Sound Bite Has No Teeth

Today, people talk in "sound bites" and they try to project an "image." But that's often not what integrity does. Integrity doesn't worry about sound bites and image. It does what's right no matter what.

Politics Ends with Ticks

Ever had a tick? They're small and sneaky, suck your blood, and get under your skin. They can spread diseases. Yep. A tick is disgusting.

It reminds me of people who "play politics." You know them. They're the ones who are always playing one person off another and checking opinions to see who has the most influence at that moment. They pretend, lie, cheat, and steal to get what they want, not really caring about anyone—well, except themselves.

A leader with integrity never plays politics.

Always Speak the Truth

Don't be a tick. Make this resolution right now to be a leader among your friends: "I will live the truth, not just talk about it."

Don't hedge on the truth. Even if it hurts, even if it costs, telling the truth is more important than getting what you want. Of course, you also don't want to use the truth like a club, battering people left and right, hurting them and then responding, "But it's the truth!" That's just mean.

Speak the truth, but do it gently, kindly, as Jesus did.

5
Change:
Without Losing Your Mind

Put yourself in this situation:

A friend says she has to tell you something you're not going to like.

Uh-oh, you think, *she's really going to let me have it.*

Your friend smiles. "It's not that bad. But the truth is, some of the kids in the group think you talk too much at our meetings. You need to let others jump in."

Oh, boy. You love to talk, but you know your friend is right.

What do you say at that point?

Try It, You'll Like It!

Change is a constant. Every day you'll have to make external changes to accommodate others, fit things into your schedule, and rearrange plans you've made. Even more difficult are the internal changes like:

☐ Ceasing to dominate the group through talking too much

☐ Fighting the urge to gossip

☐ Overcoming a bad habit

☐ Defeating a sin

But when you master the internal changes, your friends will value your leadership in their lives. Why? Because they actually see you being changed by Christ, being transformed to become more like Him. When they see you can do it through the Spirit's power, they'll believe they can do it, too. In this respect, a leader is a change agent first by changing himself or herself, then by helping others make similar changes in their lives.

Are You Resistant or Insistent?

Most people resist change. We don't want to give up habits or sins, or simply don't want to make the effort to change—even if it is for the best. What's your reason for resisting change?

"It's hard to do!"

"It may lose me some friends!"

"I'll have to change my routine."

"My shoelaces are green!"

Okay, maybe the last answer was a little far-fetched, but I've heard some pretty weird reasons people have given for not changing.

Would you change? Consider this: It's Friday night. You've invited a couple of friends over to watch videos, eat brownies and popcorn, and stay up all night. At the last minute, though, just as you stick the brownies in the oven, one of your friends calls to say her mother has surprised her by offering to take all of you out to a movie starring that really cute actor you read about all the time. What will you do? Turn off the oven and change your plans, of course! You're willing to change, because it's something you like. But what if the situation was different? What if you're now responsible for a chore you don't like? Something like picking up garbage by the roadside? How fast would that change go into your schedule?

You can't change the fact: Change will happen. When you resist it, you create another set of problems. A true leader makes the changes he or she knows need to be made—even if he or she doesn't like it!

The Good Word Gets Around

On the night I became a Christian, I knew that things were going to have to change for me. The life I lived at high school needed some radical change. I wasn't sure how I or any of my friends would handle it.

I decided that I needed to be honest and upfront with them. I couldn't play any more games. Change has to be met head-on. I immediately told my most talkative friends. I knew they would tell anyone and everyone I couldn't get to! One key student was Jack Martin, a

Doubting Thomas

We call Thomas "Doubting Thomas" because he was the lone disciple who didn't see the resurrected Jesus right away. When the other disciples told him about what had happened, he wouldn't believe unless he could put his hands in the nail holes where Jesus had been nailed to the cross. Thomas wouldn't change his opinion until Jesus appeared to him, showed him the nail holes, and proved Himself to the doubter. It was then Thomas fell at Jesus' feet, crying, "My Lord and my God!" God doesn't expect us to change our views or our lives without His input. He is willing to work with us to convince us of the truth even when we, like Thomas, might doubt it.

friend from my morning history class. I put a New Testament in my shirt pocket and talked with him—until he noticed it. Then—when he saw it—I spoke to him. Word spread. It was the smartest way I could have dealt with the change in my life.

I went on to say no to many opportunities and temptations that followed. I made decisions based on my new set of convictions—but I could because I had declared my allegiance.

Change for the Good Isn't Bad

How, then, do you make positive changes in your life and in the lives of others?

First, you have to want to! If you don't decide to change, no one can make you.

For instance, Raul enjoyed his friends Cedric and Nate. They did cool things together like build those really oversize kites that lift you off the ground—and go to rock concerts, where they always ended up in the mosh pits. A new guy named Hunter began sitting at their table, and Raul enjoyed talking to him. But when Raul wanted to include Hunter in his plans, Nate and Cedric balked. They didn't like Hunter. He talked about religion and books. They liked to talk about video games and music.

One day Raul had to make a choice: go to a rock concert with Nate and Cedric, or attend a retreat with Hunter. Raul struggled for several days trying to make up his mind. His real struggle was whether he would seek God's way or his own way. Raul finally prayed about it and realized that maybe spending all his time messing around with music and video games wasn't all that mattered. He decided to go to the retreat with Hunter.

Sometimes change is easy. Sometimes it's hard. The question to ask yourself is: IS THIS GOD'S WAY OR MY WAY?

What Makes Me Click!

Have you ever heard of the doldrums? In ancient times, when sailing ships reached a point at sea where there was no wind, no breeze at all, they were said to be caught in the doldrums. They couldn't go anywhere until either they rowed out of the area or a wind came up.

In the same way, you might think to yourself, *Do I really like the way things are going? Are things clicking in my life, or am I just sitting stuck at sea not really experiencing much that is different or great?*

If you feel that way, then change is the only way you will get out of the doldrums. Through change you will find the winds of the Spirit that can make you sail to real adventure.

How to Change without Gritting Your Teeth

How, then, do you CATCH YOUR SAIL IN THE WINDS OF CHANGE for your life and others' lives?

First, learn to trust God and then others. Can you take advice from your friends without getting angry? Can God speak to your heart without your putting up walls of resistance?

God's purpose is to make your life beautiful, not to beat you to a pulp. God doesn't push us; He draws us into His plan like a guy taking a girl's hand and running through the woods. God isn't interested in forcing you into submission. He wants you to trust Him.

Second, remember that it's easier to change

yourself than to change others. If they see you change, they'll be more inclined to try it.

Third, when you ask others to change, do it gently but directly. Don't hedge your words. Don't make excuses. Challenge them and then leave it in the hands of God.

You may be surprised to see what God will do!

Leading by Example

Deidre had gotten hooked on cigarettes. Only Vashti knew about it, and she wasn't about to tell anyone because she had the same problem. Vashti knew smoking wasn't good. She had tried to talk Deidre into quitting many times, but Deidre just laughed at her. It was true that Vashti had tried to quit smoking many times; however, within days Deidre would see Vashti smoking again. Vashti was embarrassed.

> GALATIANS 5:16: LIVE BY FOLLOWING THE SPIRIT. THEN YOU WILL NOT DO WHAT YOUR SINFUL SELVES WANT.

Finally, Vashti decided to quit. But she decided to tell no one except God. She threw her cigarettes away and hunkered down for a battle. With God's help, Vashti started fighting the urge to smoke.

After not smoking a single cigarette for a month, Vashti decided to approach Deidre. This time her advice took, though, because Deidre could see Vashti had done it. Vashti had all kinds of great advice and ideas about what to do when the "urge" hit and how she'd survived when she thought she couldn't go a second longer without a drag on a cigarette.

Because Vashti had "been there," Deidre was more willing to listen!

Vashti had led by example!

6
Mending Broken Wings

Cal had a big problem. A guy in his class, Peter, was trying to beat him up. He knew he couldn't avoid the problem forever. Someday, Peter would catch him, and he'd have to fight.

Cal went to his friend Gene and told him the problem. "I don't know what to do!" Cal said. "I don't want to fight."

WHAT WOULD YOU ADVISE CAL TO DO? WHY?

The two boys prayed. Then Gene started gathering information about Cal's problem.

"When did this start?" Gene asked.

"Monday," Cal answered.

"Do you know why he wants to fight you?"

"I don't even know the guy," Cal said.

Gene went to Cal's friends and asked them what they knew about the situation.

"I don't really know Peter, but I overheard him saying that Cal had keyed his car at the game over the weekend," said one of Cal's friends. "But that doesn't sound like Cal, and I know he and his family were out of town."

Gene went back to Cal with what he'd learned. The boys decided that CONFRONTING PETER BY THEMSELVES WOULD BE A BAD IDEA. So, Gene and Cal went to the band director, Mr. Bennett, and explained the situation. Mr. Bennett had Gene, Cal, and Peter meet in his office. Mr. Bennett listened to Peter's side and to Cal's side. When Peter heard Cal was not even in town that weekend, he apologized.

Mr. Bennett explained that after he talked with Gene and Cal, he'd called the administration about campus security. He'd learned there had been some vandalism problems around the campus. Gene, Cal, and Peter decided to work together with campus security to create a campus club like the Neighborhood Watch program.

I've Got So Many Problems—What're Yours?

Everyone faces problems—big ones, little ones, medium-sized ones. In the midst of your problems, remember: If you're a Christian, you have the greatest problem-solver of all time to help you solve your problems and those of your friends.

Making Problems Go Away the Right Way

I've found a five-step program to help me solve problems wisely. I do the following:

1. Identify the problem.
2. Ask the right questions.
3. Talk to the right people.
4. Get the facts.
5. Get involved and help find a solution.

IT WORKS LIKE THIS:

1. **Identify the problem.** Figure out what the problem really is.

Gene helped identify Cal's problem by zeroing in on the real problem: Not that Cal may be in a fight (although that would be a problem), but that the reason for the fight would have been Peter's incorrect information.

2. Ask the right questions. By asking the right questions, you can figure out the real problem.

As Gene listened to his friend Cal, he asked questions, too. Why did this guy want to fight Cal? Had Cal ever done anything to him?

3. Talk to the right people. It's true: There is wisdom in asking the opinions of many people. This helps you gain many perspectives and may lead you to consider the problem from a new angle.

Gene went to several of Cal's friends and asked them about Cal's problem. One of them may have observed something about Cal or the situation.

4. Get the facts. As you study the situation, you find out what's really beneath the surface.

Gene had to question and search a little, but in the end he got the facts and was able to help his friend.

Jesus and Those Tricky Pharisees

JESUS HAD A UNIQUE ABILITY TO SOLVE TRICKY PROB-LEMS. CONSIDER THE SITUATION HE FACED IN MARK 12:13–17. THE JEWISH LEADERS WANTED TO TRAP JESUS. SO THEY FIGURED THE WAY TO DO IT WAS TO SEND SOME PHARISEES AND SOME MEN FROM THE GROUP CALLED HERODIANS TO JESUS. (THE GROUPS HAD BANDED TOGETHER BECAUSE THEY BOTH HATED JESUS.) THE TRICK WAS TO CATCH JESUS SAYING SOMETHING WRONG.

THEY APPROACHED JESUS AND SPRANG THEIR TRAP, ASKING JESUS IF IT WAS RIGHT TO PAY TAXES. OF COURSE, EVERYONE KNOWS THAT IF YOU DON'T PAY TAXES, YOU'LL GET INTO TROUBLE. BUT CAESAR WAS NOT A GODLY RULER, SO THE JEWISH LEADERS DIDN'T LIKE HIM AND DIDN'T WANT TO PAY TAXES TO HIM. THE PROBLEM WAS THAT IF JESUS ANSWERED, "YES, PAY THEM," ALL THE JEWS WOULD REJECT HIM. BUT IF HE SAID, "NO, KEEP YOUR MONEY AWAY FROM CAESAR," THEN THE FOLLOWERS OF CAESAR WOULD HAVE JESUS ARRESTED AND THROWN INTO JAIL. THESE TRICKSTERS THOUGHT THEY HAD JESUS DUPED. EITHER WAY, THEY FIGURED, HE WAS STUCK.

BUT JESUS OUTSMARTED THEM ALL. HE ASKED FOR A COIN AND SAID, "WHOSE PICTURE IS ON THE COIN?"

THEY ALL KNEW: CAESAR'S.

THEN JESUS SAID, "GIVE TO CAESAR THE THINGS THAT ARE CAESAR'S. AND GIVE TO GOD THE THINGS THAT ARE GOD'S."

WHOA! HE SOLVED THE PROBLEM AND ALSO GOT OUT OF THE TRAP. WHAT A GENIUS!

REMEMBER THAT GENIUS LIVES IN YOUR HEART, TOO. SO HIS GENIUS IS AVAILABLE TO YOU WHEN YOU HAVE A PROBLEM TO SOLVE.

5. Get involved and help find a solution.

Don't leave your friend on his own. Volunteer to step in and give help as you can.

Gene offered Cal real help by praying with him, listening, giving advice, and helping uncover the facts. And what else did he do that was really smart? He got help when he knew the situation needed adult intervention. All good leaders get help when they need it.

MATTHEW 6:33: THE THING YOU SHOULD WANT MOST IS GOD'S KINGDOM AND DOING WHAT GOD WANTS. THEN ALL THESE OTHER THINGS YOU NEED WILL BE GIVEN TO YOU.

Hey, who else followed the five steps? If you guessed Mr. Bennett, you're right. And not only did Gene help solve Cal's problem, he got Cal and Peter interested in problem-solving in a productive manner, too.

7

Attitude Determines Altitude

Zach stood in the hall fuming.

His friend Ben walked up to him and asked what was wrong.

"The teacher told me to get out of class. I can't stand her."

Ben knew this teacher. Mrs. Apple was a hard-liner, but she was fair.

"What did she say you did wrong?" Ben asked.

"My attitude. It's always attitude! So what if I'm a little sarcastic? I'm just joking around. She said, 'Serious things require serious attention.' I think it's stupid. Shakespeare is a jerk."

Ben nodded. He didn't especially like Shakespeare, either. Too highfalutin for him. But he knew a bad attitude when he saw one.

"She's right," Ben said.

"What?"

"You do have a bad attitude."

"I'm just teasing. Can't anyone take a joke?"

"You always say that, Zach. But it's not true. You're not teasing or joking," Ben said, and started off toward the gym.

Some Key Christian Attitudes

- Love (1 Corinthians 13:1–13)—without love, you're wasting your time.

- Gentleness (Galatians 5:22–23)—it makes people trust you.

- Faithfulness (Luke 16:10–12)—it's why people trust you.

- Hopefulness (Jeremiah 29:11)—it keeps things going right.

- Forgiveness (Matthew 18:22)—it offers a new start.

- Happiness (Psalm 1:1–3)—it makes life more fun.

"You're as much of a pain as she is!" Zach called.

Ben knew it was probably a lost cause. Zach always had a bad attitude about everything. And it cost him plenty. But Zach didn't realize it. Ben knew Zach was smart and capable, but Zach had been passed up as student council representative and for a scholarship to space camp—all because of his bad attitude.

Remember: Your attitude will determine your altitude. That is, how you feel about things will determine how far you go in life.

Setting Them Up or Upsetting Them!

Attitude determines just about everything in life:

- ☐ Feel like giving up, you probably will.
- ☐ Decide to hang in there no matter what, you probably will.

- ☐ Work with the team, the team will probably work well.
- ☐ Believe life has given you a bad deal, you'll probably end up in a bad spot.

Having the Right Attitude Can Take You Far

Isaac wanted a part in the senior musical, but he believed the teachers always gave the best parts to the class stars. "I'll never get anything," he told Yolanda one afternoon.

Yolanda said, "Hey, look, why don't you tell yourself you can do it anyway? Like in the *Little Engine That Could.* Remember him? 'I think I can, I think I can.' Tell yourself that, and maybe it'll happen."

Isaac decided to try it. As he tried out for a part, he sang his heart out and told himself, "I can and I will," all through it.

Funny. He got the part. And he did a great job. His changed attitude worked wonders.

Bad Attitude Goes Right

Gideon was a guy with a bad attitude. He felt that God had let Israel down. The Midianites had taken everything, and Gideon just managed to hide some grain in a wine press. It was there, though, that God spoke to him. God told Gideon he wanted him to deliver His people (Judges 6:11–40).

After a while, Gideon began gathering an army of men to fight the Midianites, but he still had doubts. Did God really want him to fight Midian? One night, he prayed to God and laid some wool on the floor. He told God that if it was God's plan for him to fight, then in the morning he would find dew on the wool but the ground would be dry.

God did it. But Gideon still had doubts. The next night Gideon decided to try it the opposite way. This time the ground would be wet, but the wool dry.

Again, God came through.

Gideon was so encouraged, he went out and eventually defeated one hundred twenty thousand Midianites with only three hundred men. When Gideon changed his attitude, he went out and accomplished amazing feats.

How to Get a Positive 'Tude!

How do you change your attitude? These six steps work for me:

1. **Identify problem feelings.** Figure out what's wrong with your attitude and decide those are the areas you'll change. Are you bitter because some other girl got the lead role in your school play? Do you have a grudge against that boy who got to go to your club's state meeting, when you really wanted to go?

> "THE PROBLEM IS NOT THE PROBLEM, THE PROBLEM IS YOUR ATTITUDE ABOUT THE PROBLEM."
>
> —UNKNOWN

Do you think God could never use you to change anyone's life? Gideon needed to believe God would lead him to victory, so he identified his doubts and then proceeded to work through them.

2. **Identify problem behavior.** Figure out what kinds of things you're doing wrong.

What do you do that makes you feel bad about yourself? Do you say negative things about your classmates, teachers, parents, brothers, sisters? Do you act in a mean way toward someone? Do you ignore people you don't like? Do you avoid talking to people because you're concerned they won't like you? If you don't know what you're doing that's a problem, ask a good friend. Encourage him or her to be honest, and I guarantee your friend will help. Gideon knew his attitude was probably wrong, so he went to God and worked on it.

> PHILIPPIANS 4:8:
> BROTHERS, CONTINUE TO THINK ABOUT THE THINGS THAT ARE GOOD AND WORTHY OF PRAISE. THINK ABOUT THE THINGS THAT ARE TRUE AND HONORABLE AND RIGHT AND PURE AND BEAUTIFUL AND RESPECTED.

3. **Identify problem thinking.** What kinds of things go through your head that stymie you? *I'm dumb; I can't do it; I'll never succeed.* Look at those things for what they are and decide not to let them color your attitude. Gideon saw that he was afraid, so he went to God for help.

4. **Identify right thinking.** Figure out what is the best way of looking at something. *I can do it. We can succeed together. If we don't give up, we will win.* Gideon trusted God, so he proceeded on to victory.

5. **Make a public commitment to right thinking.** Let others know what you've decided to do. Gideon told Israel he had a plan, and he had a way to defeat the Midianites.

6. **Develop a plan for right thinking.** If you can, write it down. Include the positive things you'll think, the positive ways you'll act, and what you'll do to chase away problem

Keeping Your Attitude Right

- ☐ Speak words that empower.
- ☐ Read books that encourage.
- ☐ Listen to CDs and tapes that build up.
- ☐ Hang out with people who are positive.
- ☐ Pray for God to lead you.
- ☐ Work at your attitude to keep it right.

behavior and thoughts. God will help you get the right attitude fixed in your heart.

Bad habits and bad attitudes are like termites. Let them into your basement, and soon your whole house is falling down.

Work on your attitude. As you develop the right attitude, you will find that things begin to go right in ways you never expected.

8
Relationships:
High Friendship
Value = High Return

What is a friendship but a relationship? Good relationships make life worth living, for it is through relationships that we grow as people, learn to trust and love, and become who we were always meant to be. That's why a key element of being a leader as a friend is building relationships. It's considered leading by PERMISSION. Your friends and others want you to lead.

Building relationships that you value gives you a high return in terms of what you actually get out of the relationships. Of course, the main thing Jesus was concerned about was giving to others rather than getting from them. But even as you give, you get many things in return:

- ☐ Love
- ☐ Trust
- ☐ Someone to laugh at your jokes
- ☐ Someone to cry in your pain
- ☐ A listening ear
- ☐ A watchful eye
- ☐ A ready smile

Giving those things (and receiving those things) is worth more than riches and honor.

Build with the Right Materials—Love and Care

How, then, do you begin building great relationships so that you can lead as a friend?

The first thing I'd suggest is to learn to be an encourager. Think about the last time someone complimented you on something. Didn't you turn it over and over in your mind, savoring the words and telling yourself how true it was?

Sure. Encouragement encourages!

God Values Us

If you've never thought much about how valuable your relationships are, consider how much God values you:

▢ You will reign with Him. (Revelation 3:21)
▢ Your name is written in heaven. (Luke 10:20)
▢ He has forgotten all your sins. (Isaiah 43:25)
▢ You have a unit in His heavenly hotel. (John 14:1–3)
▢ Anytime you cry, He keeps a list of your tears. (Psalm 56:8)
▢ Jesus died for you. (1 Peter 2:24)
▢ He considers you His friend. (John 15:14)

Wow! If God feels this way about you, how should you feel about and value the friends in your life?

Think about how you feel when people say things like this to you:

- "Yo, that was fantastic. You did a great job."
- "Man, I could never do something like that. You're the best."
- "Thanks for helping out. You made things go smoothly."
- "You know, I think you've improved at that a hundred percent!"

Don't such words make you feel worthwhile? You can be an encourager simply by letting those compliments hang out everywhere. I once heard about a guy who was leading as a friend, and he was always "checking up" on his Christian friends to make sure they'd done their quiet time that morning, or made it to chapel, or whatever. If they hadn't done what he thought they should, he'd be very critical—even if they had, he would say they could do it better next time. He became known as Joe Checkup, and people avoided him because they knew what he was about to say.

Joe Checkup, though, realized this wasn't

very good so he changed his course. He became Joe Encourager and everywhere he went he had words of encouragement for others. Soon, people were no longer avoiding him but looking forward to him stopping by.

Encouragement is simple. Just think of something good, uplifting, or helpful to say. And then say it.

Not Just Cogs in a Machine, But the Gears That Drive It

Ever heard the expression "He's just a cog in the machine"? A cog is the little nub of metal on a gear that makes things run. It's not very pleasant thinking of yourself as just a cog. But every part of a machine has a specific job. It serves the purpose it was created for. It may be a cog, it may be a gear, it may be a bolt. No one part is more important than the others. I can prove it! The machine won't work right if even one of those parts is missing. If each of those parts is in place and in good repair and doing its job, then the whole machine works well.

And people are like that. God created each of us to do a job as part of the machine of His universe, and if everyone does the job he or she was created for, no one has to feel like "just a cog."

That's part of your job as a leader. Help people find out where they fit, what they can do to make things happen in their world.

For instance, in the movie version of the musical *The Music Man*, the main character starts out as a con artist. He convinces all the townspeople they need a band for their children, then he sells them instruments and plans to skip town with their money. But instead the attitude of the people changes him. Even after they learn

1 CORINTHIANS 12:21-22: THE EYE CANNOT SAY TO THE HAND, "I DON'T NEED YOU!" AND THE HEAD CANNOT SAY TO THE FOOT, "I DON'T NEED YOU!" NO! THOSE PARTS OF THE BODY THAT SEEM TO BE WEAKER ARE REALLY VERY IMPORTANT.

of his plan they still want him to stay and lead the band, which is surprisingly good because of his encouragement. He's found his place in the world. It changes his whole life and the lives of the townspeople for the good—all because of an attitude change.

When you show your friends how they fit into God's plan in God's world, you're helping them immensely. Remind your friends of their special talents and abilities. Point out to them what they do well and encourage them to continue working with that talent to develop it. That's how the best leaders get people to do great things in governments, corporations, and other organizations. It's how you will help your friends soar.

> "A TRUE FRIEND IS SOMEONE WHO THINKS THAT YOU ARE A GOOD EGG EVEN THOUGH HE KNOWS THAT YOU ARE SLIGHTLY CRACKED."
>
> —**BERNARD MELTZER,** LAW SCHOOL PROFESSOR

We Sail the Sea of Humanity in Relation Ships

My earliest relationship lessons came from my dad. I was a young teenager when I started to notice his masterful people skills. When we went to summer camp meetings, I would watch him talk with others and encourage them. He would walk slowly through the crowds, lifting everyone's spirits. Once I timed him as he strolled across the yard in front of the dining hall. I was in a hurry to get to the pool. It took him forty-five minutes to take a five-minute walk—because he would stop and make everyone feel like the most important person in the world. It was at that time that I went from frustration to admiration for him. My impatience gave way as I saw what his patience did for others.

I wanted so much to learn those same skills that I approached him, as a teenager, and asked if he would put me through a Dale Carnegie course on relationship skills. He not only did, but also went through it with me—as if he needed to improve! It was during those days that I learned that making people feel special really motivates them.

Finding That Niche

Lew had a good friend in Joel, but Lew was worried about him. Joel did nothing but play video games after school, before school, in the evening, whenever he had a minute. Lew knew Joel's grades were slipping and his chores weren't getting done, but he didn't seem to care.

Then one day Lew had an idea: Why not get

Joel interested in doing something he was already interested in?

"Hey, Joel," Lew said one day as they stepped onto the bus. "There's a new company in town that does computer stuff."

"Yeah," Joel said, not very interested.

"Yeah. They develop games for the computer, and they're looking for people to test them out."

"Really?" Joel said, raising his eyebrows with interest.

"Yeah. And they pay for it, and they're willing to train people to work for them in creating video games."

> "BY CONSTANT SELF-DISCIPLINE AND SELF-CONTROL YOU CAN DEVELOP GREATNESS OF CHARACTER."
>
> —GRENVILLE KLEISE, AUTHOR

"Cool," Joel said. "Maybe I'll check it out."

That little seed planted a tree because the next week Joel had a part-time job reviewing video games, and he was on his way to learning how to program new games. For Joel to be able to keep the job, his parents insisted his grades stay high and his chores be done. Soon, Joel was on the honor roll, and his chores were getting done.

Leading as a friend often means helping your

friends find their niche, the place they can fit in, and do something worthwhile with their lives.

May I Give You a Hand?

Sometimes we all fall and we all need help. Watch your friends for temptation areas. When they fall, don't club them with condemning words. Offer them a hand to get them back on their feet (and accept a hand, if it's offered to you).

Remember Galatians 6:1: "Brothers, someone in your group might do something wrong. You who are spiritual should go to him and help make him right again. You should do this in a gentle way. But be careful! You might be tempted to sin, too."

This verse points out the process of working to help restore someone who has gone off the track. How do you do that?

☐ Go to him privately.

☐ Speak gently.

☐ Remind yourself that you, too, make mistakes.

Leading Them Back to the True Path

Shelley and Jean had a great friendship. But as they got older, Shelley began to mix with the wrong kids. Jean stuck with the youth group and kids who were Christians. But Shelley strayed from her faith.

One evening Shelley invited Jean on a double date with two cute, older boys Shelley had met recently. The girls told their parents they were going to get a pizza, then see a movie. But to Jean's surprise, the boy who was driving didn't head toward the pizza place; he headed toward a dark road! When Jean objected, Shelley told her to relax, that they were going to have fun that night. Then the boys laughed and passed Shelley a bottle of whiskey, which she promptly turned up and started drinking.

Jean told Shelley and the boys that she didn't want any part of what they were doing and demanded that they take her back home. "Oh, come on," Shelley said. "Just once, don't be so righteous!"

"I mean it, Shelley," Jean said. "This is dangerous, it's against the law, and we could get in big trouble. I'm not doing this! Tell them to take us home!"

"Oh, take her home, Zeke. She's just going to ruin everything," Shelley told the boy who was driving. Angrily, Zeke spun the car around and sped back toward town. When they got to Jean's street, he slammed on the brakes at the corner and yelled, "Nice meeting you!"

JOHN 3:16: FOR GOD LOVED THE WORLD SO MUCH THAT HE GAVE HIS ONLY SON. GOD GAVE HIS SON SO THAT WHOEVER BELIEVES IN HIM MAY NOT BE LOST, BUT HAVE ETERNAL LIFE.

"Please, Shelley, come home with me," Jean whispered. "Don't go alone with them. You don't know them!" But Shelley wouldn't leave the car, so Jean, crying, walked home by herself.

The next morning, Jean got a phone call from Shelley's parents. Shelley was in the hospital. Someone had dumped her, unconscious, on their front porch in the middle of the night, then left. When the paramedics got Shelley to the hospital, her parents discovered she had drunk so much whiskey that she suffered alcohol poisoning and was nearly dead when they found her.

Jean visited Shelley in the hospital. Jean thought long and hard about what to say to Shelley that might turn her around, but she didn't want to come across as mad or condemning.

When Jean sat down, Shelley said with contempt, "I suppose you're going to tell me I shouldn't drink or hang around with the *wrong* people."

Jean shrugged. "No, I wasn't going to say that."

"Then what were you going to say?"

Jean smiled. "That I love you. That's all. That I love you."

Shelley stared at her. Suddenly, her eyes filled with tears. "I'm sorry," she said. "I know everyone who tells me how bad I've been is right, but you're the only one . . ."

She didn't finish the sentence, and Jean looked up. "The only one?"

"The only one who seems to care about me."

That night, Jean and Shelley prayed that they'd start looking out for each other and listen to each other in the future when they were tempted to do something that was wrong.

It's not always easy to do, but love never fails

to help others. It might not win the first battle or the second, but it will win the war.

The Relationship of Relationships

The most important relationship you have is the one between you and God. When He's in your life, He can guide you, encourage you, and even love you in ways no one else can. He can be the best friend you will ever have. How can you begin building a great relationship with Him? There are several things you can be doing to put God first and create a relationship with Him that is valued, worthwhile, and uplifting.

Read God's Word. Even if you read only a few verses, take the time to do this or you'll miss a great blessing—God speaking to your heart.

Pray daily. Tell God about your fears, troubles, joys, and hopes. He wants to hear them all. And tell Him about other people you want Him to bless.

Get involved in fellowship. Hang around other Christians so you can learn about God and truth.

Join a church. Volunteer to help with one of the church's ministries in some way.

This is just a starting place, but if you work at your relationship with God, you'll soon find it's not work at all, but a pure joy.

9

Discipline?
I'm Not in the Army!

Don was the type who started off great at things, but rarely finished. He went to church, got all gung-ho about having a quiet time regularly or serving with the ministry team, but after a few weeks or even days he gave up. It was too much effort.

Don's problem was self-discipline. He needed to become disciplined in order to bring into his life the things that would make him rich with love and commitment.

Do you ever see these problems in your life?

1. You want to spend time in prayer and reading God's Word, but you never seem to have the time.

2. You know you should go to the youth group at church, but there's always a movie or show you want to see at the same time.

3. You'd like to get involved in building good relationships, but deep down you're afraid people won't like you.

We all face these problems. It's self-discipline that enables us to get beyond them and start living out the things we believe in our hearts.

The Discipline That Builds Disciples

The best level of leadership is **PRODUCTION.** To lead by production, you get results! To get results, you've got to be organized. Have you misplaced your keys? Or a jacket you need? Or a schoolbook? Always keep your keys and jacket in one place. Easier said than done? Not if you build a disciplined lifestyle! How do you do that?

Don't wait, start today. Discipline begins in the present, the now. You can't constantly put it off till tomorrow because tomorrow it will be easier to put it off again. Suck in your gut and start doing now what you know is right.

Don't bite off too much at first. Don't try to do everything at once. Start with a few major disciplines like having a quiet time regularly and serving in the youth group. Stay with them and add to that foundation after they're firmly in place.

Organize yourself. Get the various aspects of your life in order through a schedule and other devices that will keep you moving ahead.

You can do this with your whole life. Think about how to plan your day, your week. Put events on your schedule so you won't forget. You're responsible for everything in your life from making sure tomorrow's jeans are clean and ready to wear to getting that science project done on time.

Remember: If you fail to plan, you plan to fail. Get things in order. Take time to organize your desk, your room, your locker. Refuse to let everything sink into a murky mess.

As your friends see you get organized, they'll want to know how you did it and they'll be amazed at how much more time you have for fun things.

☐ Set your priorities or they'll be setting you.

☐ Remember what we talked about in chapter 3 on priorities? Make a TOP TEN list of things to do, put them in the right order, and then hop to it. You'll find you'll accomplish much more by having priorities.

☐ Get your goals lined up and work toward them. Hey, come to think of it, what are your goals? What do you want to accomplish this year? It can be anything, so long as it's what you want to do. The story of the man who ran around doing everything except what really mattered is a sad one. What matters to you? To God? Get those things on your schedule, and in a year's time you'll see all you've done for His Kingdom and glory and your advancement.

☐ Do one thing at a time.

There's a story of a farmer who started to plow his field, but on the way he noticed that a post in the fence had broken. He walked to the barn to get a hammer and nail to fix the post when he saw that the pigs hadn't been slopped. He turned around and started for the food, when he saw the mail had come. He was on his way to get the mail when . . .

Well, you get the picture. Sometimes people let themselves be diverted by a million things, and they never get any one thing done. But concentrate on the one that's most important, and you'll get it done. Then move to the next thing on your list.

Don't keep everything to yourself. Share with friends what's going on in your life. What good things are happening? What's going wrong?

Report in. One of the best ways to grow is by having an accountability partner. This is someone who will ask you the hard questions and will want to know whether you're getting done the jobs you need to get done.

GALATIANS 5:22–23: BUT THE SPIRIT GIVES LOVE, JOY, PEACE, PATIENCE, KINDNESS, GOODNESS, FAITHFULNESS, GENTLENESS, SELF-CONTROL.

A Daily Fifteen-Minute Chat with God

Maybe you call your best friend daily, or make sure you see your friends before or after classes. Do the same with God. Each day, put aside fifteen minutes to be with God. It can be in the mornings, after school, at a park, when you go to bed. But it's your fifteen-minute quiet time with God.

1. **Read the Bible,** for at least five minutes. Just read. You might want to read through a whole book over several sessions. Don't just flip it open, though. Be systematic. You can read through the whole Bible, if you stick with it.

2. **Meditate on God's words.** Ask questions: What is God saying to me in this passage? What things should I put into practice that were mentioned in the passage? Should I memorize a verse that jumped out at me?

3. **Pray.** Pray for yourself, your family, your friends, your church, your school. Be as specific as you can. You can even write your prayers in a journal.

The Main Things

The main things God has used to solidify our relationship are things I can touch and see and involve myself in, such as reading the Bible and memorizing it. The way God works and the way He specifically speaks to me through His Word have been invaluable.—**Jennifer Knapp**, a gospel musician (as quoted in *Brio Magazine*)

He or she will not hesitate to ask you things like:

- Are you having your quiet time?
- Are you serving the Lord somewhere?
- Are you growing in Christ?
- Are you helping others?

This person will keep you going in the right direction.

Jesus Had the Time for Us

Ever notice that Jesus never acted angry or put off when people interrupted Him? He was always ready to take a detour to help. Why was this? I believe it was because Jesus was disciplined in all areas of His life.

We started this chapter with Don, the undisciplined oaf. Do you know what happened? Don decided to begin putting leadership principles to work in his life. In time, he became the one others looked to when they needed a job done, help with a project, or just a word of encouragement. Don had time for people because he made himself take the time with the other things.

Your friends will notice when you begin to develop discipline in your life. Why? Because you'll actually be doing good things, lasting things. Self-discipline is the foundation. But all these other principles—maintaining priorities, building relationships, keeping your integrity—will turn you into the kind of leader your friends will gladly follow.

Use these principles of leadership, and I guarantee you will be the kind of friend all of us would want to have.